D1161762

Your Guide to Government

How is a government elected?

Susan Bright-Moore

Crabtree Publishing Company

www.crabtreebooks.com

Crabtree Publishing Company

www.crabtreebooks.com

Author: Susan Bright-Moore
Coordinating editor: Chester Fisher
Series editor: Scholastic Ventures
Project manager: Kavita Lad (Q2AMEDIA)
Art direction: Dibakar Acharjee (Q2AMEDIA)
Cover design: Ranjan Singh (Q2AMEDIA)
Design: Tarang Saggar (Q2AMEDIA)
Photo research: Anju Pathak (Q2AMEDIA)
Editor: Molly Aloian
Proofreader: Crystal Sikkens
Project coordinator: Robert Walker
Production coordinator: Katherine Kantor
Font management: Mike Golka
Prepress technician: Ken Wright

Photographs:
Cover: Adam Bird/Associated Press, J. Helgason/ Shutterstock (background); Title page: Ariel Skelley/ Jupiterimages; P4: Joe Raedle/Staff/Getty images; P5: Joe Cavaretta/Associated Press; P6: Justin Horrocks/ Istockphoto; P7: Phil Portus/Alamy; P8: Marcel Mooij/ Shutterstock; P9: Alex Wong/Staff/Getty images; P10: Kathy DeWitt/Alamy; P11: Rogelio Solis/Associated Press; P12: SCPhotos/ Alamy; P13: Daniel Rodriguez/ Istockphoto; P14: Mtrommer/Bigstockphoto; P15: Charles Krupa/Associated Press; P16: Dennis MacDonald/Alamy; P17: Joshua Lott/Stringe/Getty Images; P18: Amanda Haddox/Shutterstock; P19: HO Old/Reuters; P20: Brad Rickerby/Associated Press; P21: Penny Violet-Gee/Alamy; P22: Marc/Flickr; P23: Charlie Neibergall/Associated Press; P24: Jim Young/ Reuters; P25: Laura Rauch/Associated Press; P26: Pictorial Parade/Staff/Getty Images; P27: W. Eugene Smith/Stringer/Time & Life Pictures/Getty Images; P28: Eric Draper/Mai/Contributor/Time & Life Pictures/ Getty Images; P29: David Zalubowski/Associated Press; P30: Stefan Klein/Istockphoto; P31: David Young-Wolff/Alamy

Library and Archives Canada Cataloguing in Publication

Bright-Moore, Susan
    How is a government elected? / Susan Bright-Moore.

(Your guide to government)
Includes index.
ISBN 978-0-7787-4325-5 (bound).--ISBN 978-0-7787-4330-9 (pbk.)

    1. Elections--United States--Juvenile literature. 2. Voting--United States--Juvenile literature. 3. United States--Politics and government--Juvenile literature. I. Title. II. Series.

JK1978.B75 2008   j324.60973   C2008-903652-2

Library of Congress Cataloging-in-Publication Data

Bright-Moore, Susan.
    How is a government elected? / Susan Bright-Moore.
        p. cm. -- (Your guide to government)
    Includes index.
    ISBN-13: 978-0-7787-4330-9 (pbk. : alk. paper)
    ISBN-10: 0-7787-4330-6 (pbk. : alk. paper)
    ISBN-13: 978-0-7787-4325-5 (reinforced library binding : alk. paper)
    ISBN-10: 0-7787-4325-X (reinforced library binding : alk. paper)
    1. Elections--United States--Juvenile literature. 2. Voting--United States-- Juvenile literature. 3. United States--Politics and government--Juvenile literature. I. Title. II. Series.

JK1978.B75 2008
324.60973--dc22   2008025369

Crabtree Publishing Company

www.crabtreebooks.com   1-800-387-7650

Published in Canada
Crabtree Publishing
616 Welland Ave.
St. Catharines, ON
L2M 5V6

Published in the United States
Crabtree Publishing
PMB16A
350 Fifth Ave., Suite 3308
New York, NY 10118

Published in the United Kingdom
Crabtree Publishing
White Cross Mills
High Town, Lancaster
LA1 4XS

Published in Australia
Crabtree Publishing
386 Mt. Alexander Rd.
Ascot Vale (Melbourne)
VIC 3032

Contents

What is an Election?

An **election** is a time when many people vote for our **goverment's** laws and leaders.

What is a government? A government is a group of people who have the power to make rules or laws for an area. A government can be small such as a city council, or it can be big such as the United States Congress. There are many types of governments. The United States has a special kind of government called a **democracy**. In a democracy, the people help make decisions by voting.

This woman is casting her vote in an election.

When people run for **office**, they try to get as many people to vote for them as possible.

Think about a family planning a vacation. Everyone shares their ideas. Each family member votes on where to go.

Democracy works this way, too. People choose the leaders.

We discuss how we feel and then we vote. The person who receives the most votes wins! You need to choose your leaders carefully. Do some homework. Find out what the leader believes in and promises to do. This will help you choose wisely.

The Right to Vote

Who is able to vote in an election?

In a democracy, everyone should have a voice. However, there are some rules about who can vote. For example, you must
- be a U.S. citizen,
- be 18 years old, and
- not be in jail.

Can you imagine being told you could not vote because you were a woman? In the past, only white males could vote. Now we know that is not fair.

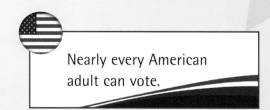

Nearly every American adult can vote.

Years ago, women were not allowed to vote.

In our country, we want everyone to be able to vote. A democracy works best when everyone can vote. But some people do not exercise their right to vote. It is important that everyone votes so that we can hear the ideas of everyone.

FACT BOX

In the past, only people who owned property could vote. Who did this leave out? How has our voting rules changed?

Why Do We Vote?

Some people do not vote, even when they have the right to vote. It is important for everyone to exercise their right to vote.

These adults should vote for laws and leaders they believe in.

We elect leaders to make decisions, but we have a job, too. Our job is to care. We have to care about who we vote for and what we vote for.

There are other ways we care for our country.

1. First, we tell what we think and believe.
2. Then, we listen to and find out the beliefs and opinions of others.
3. Finally, we vote.

But, that's not all...

What if you saw trash all over the park? You could get a group of people together to clean it.

The park gets messy again. Now what? You gather together a group of people. You write letters to the town council asking them to put trash cans in the park. The town council likes your idea and buys trash cans. Working together, people can make a difference in our country. People who vote can influence the decisions that leaders make.

Voters let people know what they want.

Who Do We Vote For?

Everyone who runs for office thinks they would do a good job. But do they agree with what voters think is important?

Who decides what is important? The voters decide what is important.

If you wanted to start a recycling program in your city, you would tell others about your idea. You might have them sign a **petition**, or a piece of paper saying they agree. If recycling is important to many people, then it goes to the election. There, everyone can vote to say if they want a recycling program.

Voters pay attention to the news in order to learn about **candidates**.

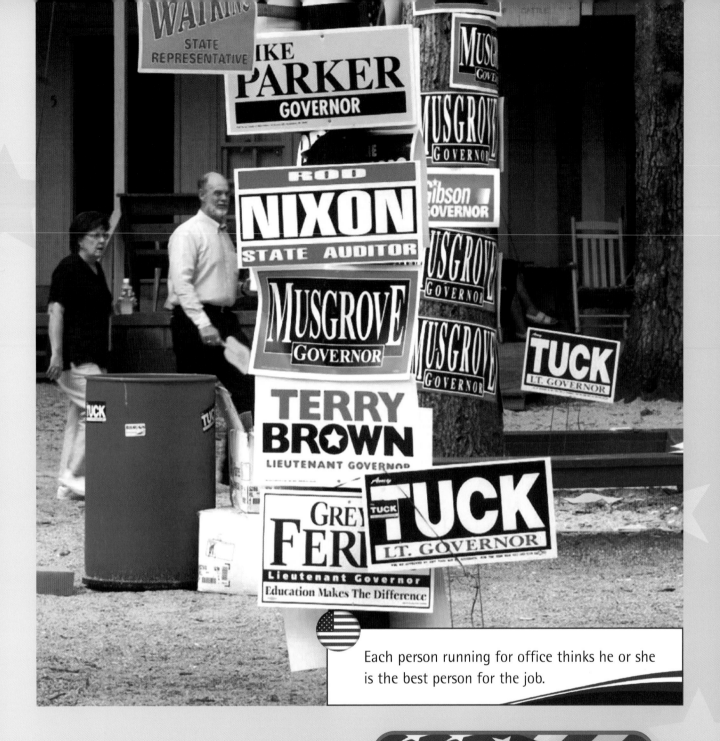

Each person running for office thinks he or she is the best person for the job.

How do you choose the best person when you have never met them?

You can read about the candidates in a newspaper or on the Internet. Candidates will often give speeches that you can watch on TV. Sometimes, they will hold special meetings where you can ask the candidates questions.

FACT BOX

Sometimes newspapers endorse a candidate. An **endorsement** means the newspaper believes that person is best for the job.

11

Different Issues

Every person is different. What each person thinks is important may be different, too.

Our country is made up of many people. Some are young, and some are old. Some work in factories, and some work in office buildings. Some are healthy, and some are sick.

Think about your family. Do you agree on everything? Do you think you should get to stay up later? Do your parents think you should clean your room more? What is important to one person may not be to another.

These people may vote for candidates who want health care for older Americans.

These workers may want candidates who want more jobs in America.

The different groups in our country think differently, too. Older people may be worried about their health. Parents may be interested in schools for their children. Do you think a person would get elected if they only talked to one group or talked about one issue? To get elected, the candidate needs to get votes from many groups. The candidate must talk about many issues and be liked by different groups of people.

Political Parties

Parties sound like celebrations. But in the government, parties are not for fun!

Sometimes groups of people with similar beliefs join together. They try to get their candidates elected. These groups are called **political parties**. They talk to people about issues and candidates. They may hold special meetings where people can ask their candidates questions.

There are two main political parties in our country. They are called the Democratic Party and the Republican Party. Have you seen their logos? The Democrats use a donkey as a logo. The Republicans use an elephant.

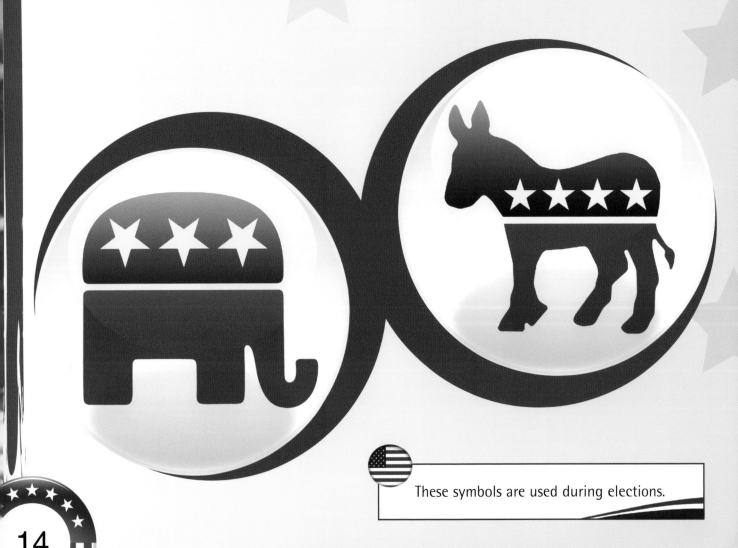

These symbols are used during elections.

PRESIDENTIAL PREFERENCE
PREFERENCIA PRESIDENCIAL

To express your preference for the person to be nominated as Democratic candidate for President, you may do **one** of the following:

- Vote for **one** candidate on this page **or**
- Vote for "No Preference" if you do not wish to vote for a candidate **or**
- Write in another name and fill in the oval to the right.

Caution: Do **not** vote for "No Preference" **and** write-in.

Para expresar su preferencia por la persona que se nombrará como candidato demócrata para la Presidencia, escoja **una** de las siguientes opciones:

- Votar por **un** candidato en esta página **o**
- Votar por "No Preference" (Ninguna preferencia) si usted no desea votar por ningún candidato **o**
- Agregar un nombre y rellenar el óvalo que tiene a su derecha.

JOHN R. EDWARDS .... ◯

HILLARY CLINTON .... ◯

JOSEPH R. BIDEN, JR. .... ◯

CHRISTOPHER J. DODD .... ◯

MIKE GRAVEL .... ◯

BARACK OBAMA .... ◯

DENNIS J. KUCINICH .... ◯

BILL RICHARDSON .... ◯

NO PREFERENCE / NINGUNA PREFERENCIA .... ◯

DO NOT VOTE IN THIS SPACE. USE BLANK LINE BELOW FOR WRITE-IN.   NO VOTE EN ESTE ESPACIO. USE LA LÍNEA EN BLANCO DE ABAJO PARA AGREGAR UN CANDIDATO.

WRITE-IN SPACE ONLY   ESPACIO EXCLUSIVO PARA AGREGAR CANDIDATO ◯

All of these candidates are Democrats who wanted to be president.

Some people follow a certain party. When they vote, they choose all the people their party supports. However, you do not have to. You can vote for any candidates you want from any party.

FACT BOX

There are many other small political parties in the United States. One small party is the Green Party. They support candidates who want to protect and care for our environment.

How to Vote

An adult cannot just walk up and ask for a **ballot**. The steps for voting start well before election day.

In order to vote, you need to **register**. The government will make sure that you are old enough and live in that area. Once you are registered, you will get a voter's registration card, which you can use to vote.

Then you need to find out when the election is held. On Election Day, you go to a special place called a **polling place.**

At the polling place, you will walk inside a **voting booth**. It is surrounded by curtains so that no one can see who you vote for.

 Signs help people find the polling place.

Voting booths have sides to keep people from seeing each other's votes.

Inside the booth, you will mark your choices on a ballot. Ballots list all the candidates and issues.

Many Elections

Towns, cities, counties, states, and our country all have governments. Each one has its own elections.

We vote for a president every four years.

18

It takes many people to run our country.

Imagine someone wants to build a road in your city. You elect leaders in your city to make those decisions. **Local** leaders are in charge of the work and decisions for their area.

What if the road went from one city to another? Since it concerns more than your city, **state** leaders would make the decisions. We elect state leaders to do the work and make decisions for the whole state.

What if the road were going to go from your state to another state? Now the federal government would be in charge. The **federal** government does the work and makes decisions for the whole country.

We have many different governments in our nation. Each level of government has responsibilities. Each holds elections. When you vote, you will elect national, state, and local leaders.

Local elections might include someone running for sherrif.

19

Vote for Me!

When a person decides to run for a job in government, how does he or she let everyone know to vote for him or her?

So how do you get elected? You run a **campaign**. A campaign is a way to let voters know about a candidate. The candidate wants people to know his or her name. The candidate also wants people to know his or her beliefs.

Have you seen a candidate on TV? Candidates work hard to get people's votes. They visit many places. They meet many people and give speeches. They appear on TV and put ads in newspapers.

Candidates talk to voters at stores during a campaign.

Big signs would get a lot of attention during a campaign.

Getting elected is a big job. Candidates need to talk to as many people as they can. To get elected, candidates use volunteers and helpers.

Volunteers do many jobs. They make phone calls to tell people about their candidate. They walk around to houses and leave information about their candidate. They stuff envelopes with information to mail out to people. These people are important to a candidate's campaign.

What is a Primary?

It takes many months for Americans to decide which candidates will run for president. There must be only one candidate from each party.

Months before the election, there are many candidates. There may be several Democrats and several Republicans running. However, as the election gets closer, only one candidate from each of the parties will be chosen to run.

This happens during the **primaries**. Each state holds a primary, which is a special election. Primaries are held from January through June.

New Hampshire always has the first presidential primary.

NEW HAMPSHIRE'S PRESIDENTIAL PRIMARY

Since 1920, New Hampshire has held its presidential primary election before any other state. Changes in New Hampshire law in 1949 made the primary a direct selection of presidential aspirants, not a mere choice of delegates pledged to specific nominees. Held in February or March, during the week preceding any similar election elsewhere, the New Hampshire primary has become a critical first step on the road to the White House. Taking their responsibility seriously, New Hampshire voters test contenders during the months leading to the primary and have usually favored the candidate who ultimately attains the Oval Office.

2000

These two candidates both wanted to win primary elections.

During the primary, the people in each of the two main political parties choose who they want to be their actual presidential candidate. This means that the Democrats are competing against the other Democrats and the Republicans are competing against other Republicans. In most states, you only vote for a candidate from your party.

FACT BOX

Each state decides how they want to elect their primary candidates. Some states hold an election. Other states elect their party candidates in special meetings called **caucuses**. What would it be like to attend a caucus meeting?

National Conventions

When the primaries are over, it is time for Democrats and Republicans to each choose one candidate.

The primaries are over. Each state has chosen the one person they want to represent each party. But what if Texas chose one person and California chose another?

This is why the parties hold **national conventions**. The Democratic and Republican Parties hold a large meeting. Each state party sends delegates to vote for the candidate that was chosen in their state.

This is a national convention. It looks like a big party, but the meetings are important.

People even wear costumes to the conventions!

The convention is fun, but it is also important. Once the party decides on their candidate, the candidate will choose a **running mate**. The running mate will become the vice president if elected.

The party also decides on its **platform**. A platform is a list of things the political party will support if their candidate is elected. A party might promise to give more money for education or lower the number of taxes people pay.

Exciting Elections

In some elections, people are able to predict the winner easily. Other elections are much more interesting.

On election night, people may gather around the TV listening to election results. Sometimes, people have a good idea about who will win. Other times, it is a big surprise. What were some of the exciting races?

- In 2000, George Bush was the Republican candidate, and Al Gore was the Democratic candidate. The election was so close that the winner was not decided until days after the election.

The debate between Kennedy and Nixon was the first that most Americans could see.

Harry Truman was elected president in 1984. Many newspapers guessed Dewey would win. They did not wait to see the actual results!

- In 1960, John Kennedy and Richard Nixon held the first debate on TV. Nearly 70 million people watched them argue about what was best for the country.

- In 1948, Harry Truman and Thomas Dewey had an exciting election night. Most people expected Dewey to win. Truman surprised people by winning the election.

FACT BOX

We hold elections every four years. A president can only be president for two terms. Why do you think we limit terms?

American Elections

Elections in the United States are different than elections in other countries.

George W. Bush ran for president in 2000, and then again four years later.

Some countries do not have elections. The people do not get to choose their leaders.

Other democratic countries hold elections. Elections work differently in these countries.

• They have different political parties. In the United Kingdom, the two major parties are the Labour Party and Conservative Party.

• They also hold elections for different jobs. Several countries elect a Prime Minister instead of a President.

Elections happen at different times. Our congresspeople are elected every four years, while in the United Kingdom, the House of Commons is elected every five years.

In the United States, we hold many elections each year because we have so many levels of government. In one year, you might vote for city, county, state, and national leaders.

People get very excited about presidential elections, because they only happen every four years!

Local elections might happen every two or four years.

Why Don't People Vote?

Voting is the way people control what happens in our government. But not everyone who can vote actually does.

After reading about the close elections and surprise elections, you can see how every vote counts. Yet, some people do not go to vote.

Why do you think people do not vote? There are many reasons. Some people think that one vote does not matter. Others just think they are too busy. Some people are not aware of the election, especially in local elections.

During election years, people work hard to encourage all voters to get out and vote.

These people know how valuable their votes are.

The National Voter Registration Act makes it easier for people to register to vote. They can even register while they get their driver's license.

Different groups educate and encourage voters to register and vote. Rock the Vote is a group that uses young people's interest in music to encourage them to vote.

FACT BOX

About three out of every ten people who could vote do not even register. The seven out of ten people who do register may not all vote!

Glossary

ballot Lists all the candidates and issues

candidates People wanting to be elected

caucus A special meeting where candidates are selected

endorsement When someone publically announces who they think should be elected

government A group of people who have the power to make rules or laws for an area

national convention A large meeting held by a political party to choose the one candidate they support and decide their platform

office A position or job in the government

platform A list of things the political party will support if their candidate is elected

political party A group of people with similar beliefs that try to get candidates elected

polling place The place where elections are held

register To enter your name as a voter

running mate The person the presidential candidate is choosing to run for the vice presidential position

voting booth A private area where you go to vote

Index

Printed in the U.S.A.